"I do not make films primarily for children. I make them for the child in all of us, whether we be six or sixty."

For Rotem, a flower in bloom —D.R.

To Roy E. Disney —J.P.

Text copyright © 2018 by Doreen Rappaport   Illustrations copyright © 2018 by John Pomeroy

Library of Congress Cataloging-in-Publication Data

Names: Rappaport, Doreen, author. Pomeroy, John, 1951- illustrator.
Title: Walt's imagination : the life of Walt Disney / by Doreen Rappaport ;
illustrated by John Pomeroy.
Description: First edition. Los Angeles : Disney-Hyperion, 2018.
Identifiers: LCCN 2017014810 ISBN 9781423184706 (hardcover) ISBN
142318470X (hardcover)
Subjects: LCSH: Disney, Walt, 1901–1966—Juvenile literature.
Animators—United States—Biography—Juvenile literature.
Classification: LCC NC1766.U52 D5377 2018 DDC 741.58092 [B]—dc23
LC record available at https://lccn.loc.gov/2017014810

This book is set in ITC Fenice/Monotype; Barmbrack Bold/Fontspring
First Edition, July 2018 | 10 9 8 7 6 5 4 3 2 1
FAC-029191-18145 | Printed in Malaysia
Reinforced binding

Visit www.DisneyBooks.com

Walt's Imagination

THE LIFE OF
Walt Disney

by Doreen Rappaport

illustrated by John Pomeroy

Peachtree

Disney • HYPERION

LOS ANGELES   NEW YORK

Walt wandered the family farm
and saw rabbits, foxes, raccoons,
bobwhites, crows, and cardinals.
He bottle-fed his favorite pig, Skinny,
and rode hogs into their muddy pigpens.
He put his ear to railroad tracks nearby
to hear the trains coming.
His neighbor paid him a nickel
to draw a picture of a horse.

"The result was pretty terrible, but both the doctor
and his wife praised the drawing highly."

Walt thought life in
Marceline, Missouri, wondrous.
Unfortunately, the family farm failed.
When Walt was nine,
his family moved to Kansas City, Missouri.

His father started a newspaper-
delivery business.
Walt and one of his brothers,
eighteen-year-old Roy, worked for him.
For six years, every morning at 3:30 a.m.,
Walt trudged through snowdrifts,
got drenched in rain,
and sweltered in heat.
Their father paid all the other newsboys,
but not Roy and Walt.

"After all, I clothe and feed you,"
    he told them.
    After two years, Roy quit and left home.

Walt took an extra job after school
for spending money.
He was constantly tired and
often fell asleep in class.

"I was working all the time.
I never had any real playtime."

Still, Walt found energy to draw.
When his fourth-grade teacher
told her students to draw flowers,
Walt drew a human face on them
with arms for the leaves.
His teacher was not pleased.

Walt also loved to perform.
He went to stage shows
with his friend Walt Pfeiffer.
They copied down jokes and songs
to create their own acts.
Walt sneaked out of the house at night
to perform in talent contests.
Once they won fifth prize and
twenty-five cents.

"I liked acting! Liked the applause,
liked the cash prizes, liked the weird smells
and weirder sights behind the scenes."

Walt loved acting,
but drawing won out.
A barber decorated his shop
with Walt's caricatures of his customers
and paid him in haircuts and money.

"It was a great stimulant to know my efforts
were appreciated."

In high school he was praised
for his cartoons in the school paper.
He wanted to go to art school at night.
His father agreed to pay if Walt got a job.
Walt got two jobs and
studied cartooning and anatomy.
He soon realized
he would never be a fine artist.
His talent was in caricature.

"It was the turning point in my whole career."

When Walt was sixteen,
the United States was at war.
He wanted to fight for his country
like his brothers Roy and Ray.
But he was too young.

He tried to join the Red Cross, but
his father refused to sign the papers.
He begged his mother, and finally
she signed for both parents.
She never knew that Walt changed
his birth date to make himself seventeen,
the legal age needed to join the Red Cross.

"I just had to get in there."

In France he delivered food
to bombed-out villages.
During his free time, he drew on tanks
and on helmets.
He drew caricatures of soldiers.
He sent drawings to humor magazines,
but he never sold any.

When Walt returned from France,
he dropped out of high school
to pursue his dream to be an artist.
He fell in love with animated cartoons.
He pored over photographs of
horses galloping and athletes running
so his drawings would be more realistic.

"The trick of making things move on film
is what got me."

He used his earnings from the Red Cross
to set up an animation studio.
He created a twelve-and-a-half-minute
silent cartoon about a real girl
in a cartoon world.
Alice rode an elephant in a parade.
Giraffes, rabbits, and dogs welcomed her.
She danced while a cat orchestra played.
No one bought the Alice Comedies
to show in theaters.
Walt was broke.
Roy told him to join him in California,
the center of moviemaking.
Walt packed a cardboard suitcase
with a borrowed suit, one pair of pants,
two shirts, and animation equipment.

Upon arrival, Walt convinced Roy
to set up an animation studio with him.
They worked in a garage.
Roy did the photography.
Walt did the drawings.

They sold fifty-five cartoons
about Alice and her cat, Julius,
at bullfights, horse races, the beach,
and in the jungle.
They hired more artists, including
a friend, Ub Iwerks.
Walt only drew the first six films,
but he edited every scene of every cartoon.
Moviegoers liked the Alice Comedies.

But Walt knew he had so much more to learn,
so much to improve on.

"I was ambitious and wanted to make
better pictures."

In 1927 a full-length movie with sound
came out. Moviegoers loved it.
A few cartoons had music and sound,
but the sound didn't match the actions.
Walt set out to solve this problem.
He thought up a new character,
a mouse named Mickey.
Ub refined Walt's sketch of Mickey
so he could be drawn faster.

"It all started with a mouse."

Ub provided key sketches for the
14,400 drawings for *Steamboat Willie*,
starring Mickey Mouse,
who used animals as musical instruments.
Other animators finished the drawings.

It was hard timing the music to the action,
but Walt did it.

"Music has always had a prominent part
in all our products."

Moviegoers, young and old, loved Mickey,
and so did the critics.
Walt won an honorary Academy Award
for creating him.

"It hit them with a bang."

Fan mail piled up.
Soon there were Mickey Mouse clubs, and
Mickey dolls, books, blocks, puzzles,
watches, caps, socks, shoes,
footballs, boxing gloves, dollhouses,
and comic strips in twenty-two countries.

Walt created more Mickey cartoons.
He didn't draw anymore, but
for twenty years he was Mickey's voice.

Walt decided to make other cartoons.
He and Ub dreamed up a night in a cemetery.
Ub did the animation.
As the music swelled,
skeletons floated out of the graves.
Their bones rattled as they danced
and smashed into one another.
One skeleton played a xylophone
on the ribs of another skeleton.
When dawn came, the skeletons
scurried back into their graves.
Moviegoers loved it.

Walt hired more animators and
supervised every detail in
the seventy-five Silly Symphonies.

"For each Symphony, the idea was a
different story based on music with comedy."

Walt kept thinking up new ideas.

When color film was invented,
Walt immediately wanted to use it.
Roy was against it. Color film cost so much.
Walt pushed ahead and changed
a black-and-white film, *Flowers and Trees,*
into color.
Moviegoers and critics loved it,
and it won an Academy Award.

Next Walt and his staff tackled
the folktale "The Three Little Pigs."
Artist Fred Moore gave each pig
a separate personality.

"You have to portray not only that
this thing is moving,
but it is actually alive and thinks."

Moviegoers heard huffing and puffing
as the Wolf blew down
Fiddler Pig's and Fifer Pig's houses.
But the Wolf failed to destroy
Practical Pig's house of bricks.

Moviegoers loved all three pigs
and the song they sang:
Who's afraid of the Big Bad Wolf,
the Big Bad Wolf,
the Big Bad Wolf?

Pete

Chip & Dale

Many friends were created for Mickey.
Walt and Ub created Minnie Mouse,
his girlfriend.
Pluto, the pup, was Mickey's pet.
Minnie had a dog named Fifi
and a cat named Figaro.

Three animators created Donald,
who became as popular as Mickey.
Donald was good-natured but rude.
His girlfriend, Daisy Duck,
helped cool him down.
Donald had three nephews,
Huey, Dewey, and Louie,
who were identical triplets.
Art Babbit and Frank Webb created Goofy,
Mickey's and Donald's best friend.

The cartoon shorts were great, but
Walt and Roy didn't make much money.

Walt wanted his cartoon characters
to move like real people.
Artists were hired to teach the animators
to draw better so that every action
a character made looked real.
The animators sketched live models.
They studied slow-motion photographs
of glass breaking and
bubbles forming and popping
to make these actions look real, too.

"We invested them with life."

The animators showed Walt their sketches.
Walt looked at the sketches while
the animators read the plot and dialogue
under each one.
If Walt didn't like what he saw or heard,
he raised his eyebrows, coughed,
or drummed his fingers on the table.
He made suggestions on plot and gags.
Sometimes he acted out what he wanted.
Many employees found him inspirational.
Some thought him too controlling.

Audiences loved these short cartoons.
But Walt wasn't satisfied.
He decided to do something
no one had ever done:
make a full-length color cartoon.
Everyone thought it was a bad idea.

He adapted the fairy tale
"Snow White and the Seven Dwarfs."

"I thought it was the perfect story.
It had the sympathetic dwarfs,
the heavy, the prince, and the girl."

Each motion a character made
required twenty-four drawings.
Each drawing was done in ink
on one side of a transparent sheet and
painted in watercolors on the other side.

It took hundreds of artists working three years
to make over two million drawings
for *Snow White and the Seven Dwarfs.*
A special camera was developed
to shoot the movie.
Walt looked at every drawing
and edited every scene.

Moviegoers loved *Snow White,*
and so did the critics.
Full-length cartoons were here to stay.

Walt kept coming up with new ideas.
One thousand artists and technicians
worked on *Fantasia,* which
set pictures to classical music.

Disney animators tackled *Pinocchio,*
about a puppet who became a boy,
and *Dumbo,* about an elephant with very
big ears, and *Bambi,* about a baby deer.
Clay models were made of Bambi.
Fawns were brought into the studio
so the artists could study them from all angles.

"These pictures represent a lot of work
and a lot of thought."

Critics loved *Pinocchio, Bambi,* and *Dumbo.*
Many critics, but not all, praised *Fantasia.*
Not as many moviegoers
came to see it as Walt had hoped,
but he refused to be discouraged.

Many Disney animators were unhappy.
Only Walt's name appeared
in the film credits, and
they did all the animation.
They had worked long hours without
extra pay on the four full-length cartoons.
They felt they deserved more money.
They wanted a union to represent their rights,
so many Disney employees went on strike.
Walt was angry and felt betrayed.
Even when the strike was settled,
he never forgot the incident.

In 1941 America was at war again.
Disney created training films
for the government.
These films didn't satisfy Walt's imagination.
When the war ended, the studio
made animated cartoons again.

But soon Walt was restless.
The studio was so big,
with so many employees
and so many productions.
He couldn't supervise every detail
in every film as he once had.

Walt became fascinated with miniature trains
and mastered the tools to build one.
He loved putting it together,
working on every detail,
the way he had once worked
on every detail in his films.

"What fun I am having."

He began to imagine a theme park
with a village that looked like his hometown,
Marceline, a Main Street with stores
selling Disney products,
and a narrow-gauge train that circled it.

"I'm going to build an amusement park, where
families will visit and have fun."

Roy didn't like the idea.
Amusement park operators
told him it would fail.
But Walt plunged ahead.

While Walt was working on Disneyland,
his imagination was still working full-time.

After television was invented,
millions of kids tuned in every day
to *The Mickey Mouse Club.*
They saw and heard Walt talk about
Disneyland, his work in progress.
They watched animated cartoons
and documentaries on natural history.
They learned about pioneer Davy Crockett.
And millions of kids sang his song,
Davy, Davy Crockett,
King of the wild frontier . . .
and bought coonskin caps sold by Disney.

Walt kept working on Disneyland,
dreaming up rides and places
in the past and future.
He saw families on paddle wheelers
going down a river and
people visiting a jungle
and the American frontier.
The original *Steamboat Willie*
would be shown in one of six cinemas.

"I want them to feel they are in another world."

He supervised every detail, and
many talented people worked
to make his dream come true.

Today there are twelve Disney theme
parks around the world
with many rides and many stores.

"Disneyland will never be completed.
It will continue to grow as long as there is
imagination left in the world."

IMPORTANT DATES

1901: Walter Elias Disney is born to Elias and Flora Call Disney.

1906–1910: The Disneys live in Marceline, Missouri.

1911: The family moves to Kansas City, Missouri.

1917: The family moves to Chicago.

1918: Walt serves the American Red Cross in France during World War I.

1920: In Kansas City, Walt and Ub Iwerks form Iwerks-Disney Commercial Artists, which fails after one month. They discover animation. Walt moves to Hollywood. He and Roy establish the Disney Brothers Studio. He sells the Alice Comedies.

1925: Walt marries Lillian Bounds.

1928: Walt creates Mickey Mouse and produces *Steamboat Willie*. By 1931 more than one million people are members in the Mickey Mouse Club.

1929: The "Silly Symphonies" come out.

1932: He hires teachers to give classes at the studio.

1933: *Three Little Pigs*, the thirty-sixth "Silly Symphony," is produced. Diane Disney is born.

1936: Lillian and Walt adopt Sharon Disney.

1937: Disney Studios develops a multiplane camera that gives depth to its films.

1939: Walt wins an honorary Academy Award for *Snow White and the Seven Dwarfs*.

1940: Disney releases *Pinocchio* and *Fantasia*.

1941: Disney animators unionize and strike. The United States enters World War II.

1942: *Bambi* is released.

1948: Disney Studios releases *Seal Island*, the first of the "True-Life Adventures" series and one of the earliest nature documentaries.

1950: *Cinderella* is released.

1954: Walt buys 244 acres near Anaheim, CA, to be the site for Disneyland.

1955: Disneyland opens. Walt introduces the "Mickey Mouse Club" program on ABC.

1964: President Lyndon Johnson presents Walt with the Presidential Medal of Freedom.

1965: Walt Disney Studios purchases land in Orlando, FL, for EPCOT, the Experimental Prototype Community of Tomorrow, which also leads to the creation of Walt Disney World.

1966: Walt Disney dies on December 15 at the age of sixty-five.

AUTHOR'S NOTE

Researching someone's life requires lots of reading—reading other biographies written by historians who spent years tracking down every detail about the person, and digging into primary sources: interviews, letters, diaries, or the person's autobiography if one has been written. Researching Walt Disney's life required all that and something extra special and FUN—the opportunity to view Disney's creations. What a WOW to go on the internet and see so many of Disney's animated cartoons. I laughed myself silly (an appropriate word) when viewing *The Skeleton Dance*, the first of Disney's seventy-five Silly Symphonies. Bats flew into my eyes, an owl's body swelled, and then, out of the graves came skeletons with their undulating bodies to dance the night away until dawn. I followed Alice, a real girl, as she entered Cartoonland and ran from a lion, her socks rolling up and down in fear. Disney's animations became more and more sophisticated as new techniques opened up, but his trademark humor and inventiveness were there from the very beginning, and it was joyous to view these cartoons.

I admire Walt Disney's creativity, but also his ferocious determination to follow his dreams. He refused to be stopped even when people he respected told him his ideas were impractical or too expensive. He reminds us to believe in ourselves, to find our own paths to a fulfilling life.

—Doreen Rappaport

ILLUSTRATOR'S NOTE

Most of my life has been either dreaming of working at Walt Disney Studios or living the dream. After three attempts at submitting portfolios, I was finally accepted into the studio's animation trainee program. There I began a relationship with an art form that would keep me busy and excited for the next forty-five years. I worked with some of the very artists that are pictured in this book. It was a time when the animators that worked on *Snow White and the Seven Dwarfs* were passing the torch to my generation of artists.

There was one thing that I wasn't expecting, and that was getting to know and work with Walt Disney's nephew Roy. He asked me to direct animation on the title character in "The Firebird Suite," part of *Fantasia 2000*. The Firebird was one of the most challenging characters I had ever animated, and Roy was extremely encouraging. He became a dear friend and neighbor, and his door was always open. We'd talk, joke, laugh, and even pray together. On one visit, Roy told me the story of when he had his tonsils removed and his uncle Walt came to visit him in the hospital. He was eight years old, and Walt sat down by his bedside and vividly re-created the entire story of Pinocchio. Roy lamented that when he saw the finished movie, it wasn't as good as when Walt told it to him. Roy passed away in 2009, and I miss him. It's to him and his memory that I dedicate these images of his uncle Walt.

—John Pomeroy

"Of all the things I've ever done,
I'd like to be remembered as a storyteller."